SUMMONED

SUMMONED

THE POWER OF PAIN

TRACIE HUNTER EVERS

Copyright © 2018 by TRACIE HUNTER EVERS.

Library of Congress Control Number:		2018911111
ISBN:	Hardcover	978-1-9845-5382-9
	Softcover	978-1-9845-5381-2
	eBook	978-1-9845-5380-5

All rights reserved. No part of this book may be reproduced or transmitted in any form or by any means, electronic or mechanical, including photocopying, recording, or by any information storage and retrieval system, without permission in writing from the copyright owner.

The views expressed in this work are solely those of the author and do not necessarily reflect the views of the publisher, and the publisher hereby disclaims any responsibility for them.

Scripture quotations marked NIV are taken from the Holy Bible, New International Version®. NIV®. Copyright © 1973, 1978, 1984 by International Bible Society. Used by permission of Zondervan. All rights reserved. [Biblica]

Scripture quotations marked KJV are from the Holy Bible, King James Version (Authorized Version). First published in 1611. Quoted from the KJV Classic Reference Bible, Copyright © 1983 by The Zondervan Corporation.

Unless otherwise indicated, all scripture quotations are from The Holy Bible, English Standard Version® (ESV®). Copyright ©2001 by Crossway Bibles, a division of Good News Publishers. Used by permission. All rights reserved.

Any people depicted in stock imagery provided by Getty Images are models, and such images are being used for illustrative purposes only.
Certain stock imagery © Getty Images.

Print information available on the last page.

Rev. date: 10/17/2018

To order additional copies of this book, contact:
Xlibris
1-888-795-4274
www.Xlibris.com
Orders@Xlibris.com
746048

CONTENTS

Acknowledgments xiii
Introduction xv

Stage 1   Denial 1
Stage 2   Anger 21
Stage 3   Bargaining 31
Stage 4   Depression 35
Stage 5   Acceptance 41

Come to me, all you who are weary and burdened, and I will give you rest. Take my yoke upon you and learn from me, for I am gentle and humble in heart, and you will find rest for your souls. For my yoke is easy and my burden is light.

—Matthew 11:28–30 (NIV)

This book is dedicated to a real-life hero, my son, Chad.

Chad,

When you were eleven years old, you saved your sister's life. It was the summer of 2001, and we had recently returned back to Daytona, Florida after I picked up you and Jordan from Mississippi.

We were poolside and I could not find Jordan. I was frantic, so I rushed to the edge of the pool to take a closer look because I had just seen her sitting in the shallow end of the pool.

There was something shimmering in the deep end of the swimming pool. The sun hit the water, illuminating the gold bracelet that Jordan was wearing on her right wrist, making the water sparkle, leading me straight to her. It was Jordan and she was drowning. She had enough presence of mind to stretch her hands up and out. She was submerged completely under water, but I saw her arms extended and her fingertips waving. Afterward, she said that she was on her "tippy toes." I still get chills to this very day thinking about Jordan's near-drowning. I remember feeling so helpless because I could not swim at the time, but thank God you were there playing with your friends near the side of the pool. I yelled at you to get in and get my daughter. You could swim like an Olympic freestyler. You looked up with your eyes closed as if to say a quick prayer before diving in. You swam that day and saved my baby's life.

You purchased a gift that you were too young to afford. You gave her eleven more years of life on Earth. Jordan was only eight years old, almost nine. The cost was pure love. It had always been just the two of you, so saving her was, in a way, saving a part of yourself. Thank you son for more years with our sweet girl. Her infectious laugh and offbeat humor will live within our hearts for the rest of our lives.

Also, to the countless parents who have lost their children to death, giving extra-special love and consideration to Doris Rich, Diana Riojas Guzman, Tajuana Dinkins-Little, Reginald Hunter, Debbie Steel, Annabel Valero, Sonya Butler, Gwendolyn Joy Reddix, Marla Jones, Zet Y'vette Fuller Brown, Delvalyn Adams, Christine O'Shields and Jo Ann Byers.

This is our cross to bear . . .

This book would not exist without the beautiful spirit of my daughter...

Jordan, I hope I did you well as your mother. I pray that this book is a work in which you would be proud.

Acknowledgments

Deborah Quave, my book coach
Thank you for your time and energy. In the midst of your climb, you lifted me.

Laura Mae Davis, my mother
Everyone should have a heart as gentle as yours.

Mrs. Rimmer, my high school advanced placement English teacher
I held on to your encouraging words for these many years.

Dr. Poole, my cardiac surgeon
Thank you from the bottom of my heart—literally. You are truly an Angel sent from the Heavens.

Introduction

Dear Reader,

Only God can turn your pain into fuel to give your soul the necessary energy to love after a tremendous loss. No loss is too small or too great. I experienced a devastating loss because of the death of my child. By the grace of God, I was able to use that pain to make my sphere of influence a kinder place and put some smiles on the faces of many. After my daughter's death, I started a scholarship fund in her name. Her birthday, October 16, is celebrated by our family, friends and Facebook family as *Jordan's Random Acts of Kindness Day*. I was also able to use that pain to write this book. My hope is that it will be a useful tool in helping others deal with significant loss.

You may not have buried a child, but each of us has experienced pain and loss in some form. Some have lost loved ones because of death, divorce, or the mismanagement of relationships. Some may be missing body parts secondary to failing health or sudden trauma. Some of us have lost ourselves in an effort to support and help those around us. Many people have been lost to drug addiction or gambling.

Unfortunately, the innocence of some children has been stolen by sexual predators or brutal family dictators. That child is forever lost until the grown-up version of himself or herself decides to heal.

The magnitude of the loss is not predicated on what you have lost. In each of these instances, pain is the common denominator.

If you have experienced any deficiency in your life, you will grow from the message in this book. My desire is to inspire you to use your pain as motivation to do something positive.

STAGE 1

DENIAL

Denial is the first stage of the five stages of grief. These five stages were first proposed by Elisabeth Kubler Ross in her 1969 book *On Death and Dying*.

A Biblical Name

After almost ten months of me being pregnant—no labor, no labor pains, no baby—it was time to encourage this stubborn bundle of joy to come into this great, big and scary world. It was time for Brooklyn Alexandria or maybe China Alexandria to show her lovely face. The induction of labor was scheduled on Friday, October 16, 1992. I was twenty-one years old and not completely set on what name should be given to this second child of mine.

My induction was successful, she was born and my heart was full. I already had a son, and I had just given birth to my daughter. The feeling of becoming a mother to a second child was a few steps past amazing.

Growing up, I thought I wanted to have six children. After Chad, my first child, was born, it quickly became apparent that I should have only as many children as I have hands.

After the birth of my daughter, my nurse came to my hospital bedside as I was being hypnotized by a perfect little yellow newborn. Later, I found out that my baby had yellow jaundice or more commonly referred to as jaundice. Jaundice presents as a pale, yellowish discoloration of the child's skin caused by an abnormal buildup of bilirubin. Immediately after she was born, she had to spend hours under a special light to resolve the skin issues.

I cannot, no matter how hard I try, recall the nurse's name. Besides, that was over twenty-five years ago, and I have since encountered a very traumatic event in my life, the death of a child. I remember that nurse being a middle-aged, straitlaced, Caucasian woman. She was clothed in all-white attire. I even remember she wore thick white stockings underneath her crisp white skirt.

She asked me if I knew God. I asked her if she knew God, but she ignored my attempt to be sarcastic by answering her question with another question.

The nurse asked, "What will you name her?"

I answered, "China Alexandria."

She looked disappointed. From the look on her tiny face, her attitude, and the absence of a wedding band, I concluded that disappointment had been no stranger in her life.

She retrieved a Bible from somewhere without me noticing. In those days, the hospitals had a Bible in all the inpatient rooms. They did not just take prayer out of school. The devils took the Bibles out of the hospital rooms where they were probably needed most.

I was thinking, *I know dang well this crazy lady is not about to try to read the Bible to me!*

She was just about to get put out of the room when she said softly, "If you love her, give her a chance! Give her a name that comes from the good book . . . something biblical!"

I thought, *If this woman was about to suggest that I name my baby Mary, I am about to get arrested.*

She continued flipping through the pages of the Bible like she was on some secret, savior mission, or something. Finally, she said,

"Jesus was baptized in the River Jordan . . ." That was all I heard, "Jordan, Jordan!"

All of a sudden, I inherited my own private summer. Two seconds before, I was freezing, but suddenly, I was hot, sweating like hell. It was not an uncomfortable sweat. It was warm and comforting; yet a strange, acute and obvious rise in my body temperature. I said the name aloud again. It sounded familiar. The name touched my heart like no other name had. I was no longer indecisive. I was ready to give this sweet little baby a proper name, now a biblical name.

The nurse was massaging a strand of beads with a cross. She laid it down on my bedside table and prayed an awesome prayer. The prayer was so uplifting that it really got my spiritual juices flowing.

"What religion are you?" I asked.

"I'm Catholic!" she exclaimed.

Then she said, "You're probably Baptist?"

"No, ma'am, I am nondenominational," I replied. "I belong to the Church of Christ on Meridian Street in Moss Point."

She shrugged, retrieved her beads, and headed quickly toward the door. Without even looking back at me, she said, "Call me if you need anything."

Was this heifer mad because I was not Catholic? Did she think that all black folks were Baptist? Well, I could not get upset with her. She had just named my child. Now, I had to figure out what middle name would go with the first name of Jordan.

While attempting to decide on a middle name for my baby girl, I recalled the fake name I used while attending the University of Southern Mississippi in Hattiesburg, Mississippi. Seymone was my play name in college.

I first started using the name when some weird specimen approached me on the Hub and demanded my name. The Hub was the building that housed the post office and food court on campus. It was also a popular hangout spot before, after and even during classes. One of the restaurants in the Hub was named Seymours.

One day my friends and I were hanging out on the Hub when a young man approached us. He looked me in my eyes, introduced himself, and asked for my name. We were positioned where the restaurant sign was visible over the guy's shoulder, so when he asked my name, "Seymone" fell out of my mouth. In response, my friends all burst out laughing loudly. So homeboy knew that I had given him the wrong name. Yet, every time that I would run into him on or off campus, he would shout "Seymone!"

My daughter's name was Jordan Seymone, which in hindsight, is ironic. I chose a biblical name; yet I also chose a middle name that I had used and was not my real name. The Bible is as real as it gets, and I had paired the biblical name with a fake name. Human nature is flawed! Our spiritual side, the God in us, is constantly fighting with our flesh, our pride, and our desires to impress other people.

My Facebook Post (November 11, 2012)

I used to read the Bible, now I study it praying for enlightenment. I can now relate to the story of Cain and Abel, not as a tale of two brothers, one good and one bad but as a story about me and my inner struggle. It is a fight between flesh and spirit, a struggle of wanting to do good; yet, choosing to do wrong. Help me Lord! Every single verse and chapter in the Bible is about the individual studying it and what that person needs to reach the KINGDOM. So, we must stop calling words and quoting verses and start living through the words finding strength and purpose on our individual paths.

Jordan

Jordan was one of the most beautiful babies I had ever seen, and she was mine. I could not believe it. She was an amazing spirit with curly, jet-black hair and plump cheeks. I started calling her Noonie because she was so light-skinned that she reminded me of high noon. Some even called her Sunshine. As an infant, her smile was huge. She would smile in her sleep, and I would lie next to her sometimes and watch her until I fell asleep. She was long, twenty-one and a half inches at birth. You could feel her sweet spirit, and you got a glimpse of her gentle soul whenever you looked into her big brown eyes.

Jordan was happy from the very beginning. She was always smiling, eating and hugging on folks. Until the age of three, she was a chubby baby. Then those legs grew faster than the rest of her could keep up with, and Jordan bloomed to be around six feet tall. She was always the tallest among her friends. Because she is no longer physically here, I carry all of her six feet in my broken heart. Jordan was my second child and only daughter, and she was definitely a mama's girl.

One day when Jordan was about four years old, I walked into the living room of our home in response to my son, Chad, continuously screaming for Jordan to move out of his way. When I turned the corner, I found Jordan sitting in front of the television. She was inches away from the tv screen and squinting to see the cartoons. I felt helpless and like a failure because I had not noticed that my baby was having trouble seeing. I called the eye doctor to schedule an appointment and was told that she was too young for an eye exam. When I asked why, the doctor informed me that children had to be old enough to read or at least know their alphabets to receive an exam. He was surprised when I told him Jordan could read and that she definitely knew her ABCs. Long story short, she was smart. She had her eye exam and got her glasses at the age of four.

Some people are kind to certain people, but Jordan was kind-hearted, and it showed in her everyday life. She would do anything for her friends, and she had wide-eyed compassion with genuine love for her family. She was bubbly and energetic with the biggest smile that you can imagine. When someone had a problem, she would jump right in to offer solutions.

She was definitely a talker. Sometimes I would tell her, "Just stop moving and be quiet for a minute and just breathe!" She would laugh and respond with "Ma, I can't."

My daughter was not perfect. She made mistakes, faced challenges, and was distracted at times; but, Jordan had an amazing heart and she loved God.

Jordan's Random Acts of Kindness

Around early March 2013, a couple of weeks before my daughter died, she called me.

I said, "Hello."

Jordan said, "Hey, Ma!"

I said, "What's up, lil girl?"

Jordan said, "Listen, Ma. I know what I want for my twenty-first birthday!"

I asked, "Birthday? Your birthday is seven months away. What's wrong with you? You have never requested anything for your birthday. Ever."

I was driving around San Antonio, Texas. Jordan was attending college in Mobile, Alabama. I was so taken aback that I pulled to the side of the road to finish this strange conversation.

I said, "Why on earth would you call me in March to tell me what you want for your birthday in October?"

Jordan calmly said, "Just listen, Ma. For my twenty-first birthday, that I know is in October, I want for everyone to do random acts of kindness. I plan to talk to the school counselor to see if we can do random acts of kindness campus-wide on my birthday."

I asked, "Who is everyone?" By this time, I had removed my cell phone from my ear and was staring at it. I thought that my child was losing her mind. The nerve of her to think that her birthday is that special to strangers that they would do anything for her. We eventually said our goodbyes and our I love yous and hung up. I probably stared at my cell phone, again, for another two minutes before pulling back onto the freeway and driving home.

After she died, I learned that I was not the only person whom Jordan had shared her birthday request with. She had told her best friend, Marissa. Jordan also told one of the counselors at the University of South Alabama, where she was attending school. Jordan died two weeks after she and I discussed her ideas to spread kindness on her birthday. After we buried Jordan, everyone swung into operation "random acts of kindness." The University of South Alabama fulfilled my baby's wish. They published a huge story in the school newspaper about Jordan and asked the students, faculty, and staff to perform random acts of kindness on October 16 in memory of Jordan. Hundreds of people participated online and on campus.

I asked all my family, friends, and Facebook family to perform random acts of kindness on her birthday and post it to Jordan's Facebook page. I was overwhelmed with the responses. Everyone showed up in a mighty way. I knew that my baby was smiling in Heaven. Jordan's legacy is one of kindness and love. Most twenty-year-olds look forward to their twenty-first birthday so that they can party, drink and act a fool. My baby looked forward to people spreading love by being kind to one another.

We decorated Jordan's gravesite for her twenty-first birthday. The tears were plentiful, but the decor turned out great. A large group of us gathered around her grave, and we sang happy birthday. Jordan's friend, Tawinka, sang a beautiful rendition of "He Wants It All" by Forever Jones.

I was so focused on doing random acts of kindness and preparing for her twenty-first birthday that I think my grieving process was easier than it would have been. Jordan knew I tried to give 100 percent effort to any project. Somehow she knew I would be completely focused on her birthday wish, that it would protect me from feeling the pain of her death all at once. I cannot say if she knew she was going to die, but she knew that I would need a huge distraction.

TRACIE HUNTER EVERS

ACTUAL JOURNAL ENTRY

My heart was scarred by the irreversible hurt of death. Somehow, she set me up to be protected. Somehow, she knew.

October 16, 2013

What Happened to Jordan

The date was March 19, 2013. The time was approximately 9:30 p.m. CST. I was settling into my apartment while on a business trip in San Antonio, Texas, when my cell phone rang. It was my daughter's number displayed on the screen, so I answered, expecting to hear Jordan's voice on the other end of the line. Instead, it was the voice of a stranger. The young lady on the phone was screaming and crying. Through her sobs, I heard Jordan had collapsed while playing volleyball and that the paramedics had been attempting to revive her for the last thirty-five minutes. When I asked her if my daughter had a pulse, she simply replied, "No, Ma'am." My heart sank.

Although she was calling from Jordan's phone, the young lady who called seemed to be confused as to if the lifeless body on the gym floor was Jordan or her good friend, Anna. Honestly, I was hoping that it was anyone else, just not my child.

I was in a state of shock. For me, the shock shielded my natural reaction and provided some emotional protection from hearing that my child had collapsed, had no pulse, and was not breathing. I was a registered nurse traveling the country taking care of other folks. I needed to get to Alabama to take care of my daughter.

I called the San Antonio Airport, only to be told there were no available flights left that night. The person on the other end of the phone suggested that I drive to Dallas to catch a flight if it was a true emergency. It was a three-hour drive by car. Dallas/Fort Worth International Airport usually had flights coming and going, until really late hours of the night. That was the kind of emergency where you could not drive anywhere! Not to Dallas, not even around the corner.

I was alone and stranded in San Antonio, Texas, and my daughter was in serious trouble at college in Mobile, Alabama. I started making phone calls. I do not remember all the calls I made that night, but later, I was surprised to view my cell phone call log and find that I had made over thirty calls that night.

The very first call was to my friend, Kimberly. Kim lived in our hometown of Moss Point, Mississippi, so she was only a forty-minute drive from the USA campus, where Jordan had passed out. I will never forget her response to hearing about Jordan. She said, "I am on my way there now!"

The next call was to my mother. That was a very difficult call to make, but I needed her to feel my pain and concern in that moment, and I cannot explain why. As soon as I told her what had happened to Jordan, she let out an extremely loud scream that seemed to echo through my tiny apartment. The sound pierced my soul and my conscience, simultaneously. My stepfather was there to comfort her, but I was alone.

Next, I dialed my then-husband's cell phone and woke him up from a deep sleep. It was almost eleven o'clock at night. Our home was in Gautier, Mississippi, about an hour away from Jordan. When I told him what happened, he was completely silent. The only sounds I could hear was him hurriedly getting dressed. Then I heard the car being started and the garage door opening. He was en route. He said, "I am so sorry, Baby!" and we hung up.

The next number I dialed was that of my sister, Eukeisha. I hurt her so bad that night by telling her what happened to Jordan. I felt like I needed to comfort her, and it was my child who was in trouble. Keisha is my younger sister. When she hurts, I hurt. That night was different. We were both suddenly dealing with new emotions and the uncertain outcome of the incident with Jordan. If I remember correctly, she was too distraught to drive that night. She drove to Mobile the next morning.

I remember calling my nurse manager and my nurse recruiter that night, but I do not remember those conversations.

While I was making all these calls, there were many incoming calls to my cell phone from Jordan's friends, giving me updates on her condition. After working on Jordan for over forty-five minutes, the paramedics had intubated my baby and transferred her to the intensive care unit at Providence Hospital in Mobile, Alabama.

I felt desperate yet hopeful. There was still an opportunity for God to intervene on Jordan's behalf . . . on my behalf.

Of all the calls I made that night, the most important call I made was to drop to my knees and call on Jesus. "May Your will be done, Lord, and may You give me the strength to do whatever is necessary to survive this storm. It is all on You."

I arrived at Mobile Regional Airport around noon on March 20, 2013, the day after Jordan collapsed. The airport was only a short drive to the hospital where Jordan and my family were. My ex-husband picked me up from the airport. He was visibly shaken. He kept telling me that our girl was gonna be okay.

It took a very long time to find parking at the hospital, but we finally caught someone backing out of a space near the entranceway. We got on an elevator that was full of college-age children. To my surprise, they got off on the fifth floor with us. They were all there to see Jordan. The hallway leading to the ICU was lined with students, friends, strangers and our family.

When Jordan collapsed during an intramural volleyball game in the USA campus gym, many of the students followed the ambulance to the hospital to check on and pray for her. Some of them had stayed there overnight. The magnitude of strange and familiar faces was overwhelming. My baby was in trouble, but she was loved.

I pressed the call button positioned on the wall just outside the ICU doors and announced that I, the mother of Jordan, was there. The loud buzz from the call button startled me because I had gotten zero sleep the previous night. I entered the intensive care unit and crossed the threshold of room 504 to be confronted by a new reality.

My child was propped up in bed and leaning to the left, and she had three or four drips going to her intravenous access device. I will never forget the green, plastic cooling blanket that draped her bed. She had on a hospital gown, and she was on mechanical ventilation. In other words, she was not breathing on her own. Her mouth was kept open by the breathing tube, and there was a feeding tube in her nose. I remember smelling baby lotion. There was a blood pressure cuff on her right arm, and two IV pumps were positioned behind the bed. Her eyes were half shut, but all I felt was complete emptiness as I hugged and kissed on her. She was ice cold except her cheeks, so I kept pressing my cheek to hers as I held her other cheek in my hand. I kept telling her, "Jordan, I need you. I need you. You are amazingly strong, and I need you to fight with everything in you!"

Jordan was on a ventilator for seven days. On March 20th, the second day of her hospitalization, the neurologist showed me Jordan's brain scans and told me that her brain was only functioning at 50 percent. I knew what that meant. I did not care about normal brain function. She was still living. I was determined to get her out alive even if I had to tote her around on my back for the rest of my life. I just wanted her to be vital and to continue to exist.

By the sixth day, there was zero brain activity, and Jordan was on a high-dose heparin drip because she developed blood clots in both arms and legs.

Late one night, on the sixth day, one of the nurses getting off duty stopped by the lobby where I was sleeping. She told me that she placed her Rosary on Jordan's bedside and wanted to make sure I was okay with her doing so. I told her yes and attempted to go back to sleep. I closed my eyes and thought about what the nurse just told me. It was such sweet gesture. Shortly after these thoughts passed, another thought entered my mind like a freight train. *Did she just say Rosary?*

Rosary?

Suddenly, I remembered my first encounter with a Rosary. It was with my nurse whom I had at Singing River Hospital in Pascagoula, Mississippi, when Jordan was born twenty years prior. The first nurse had placed a Rosary on my bedside table after I had given birth to Jordan. I cannot explain how, but it was this moment when I knew Jordan was not going to make it out of this hospital alive.

What was all this Rosary stuff?

I'm not Catholic! What was God trying to tell me, and why was He using Catholics to tell me? The mystery of this second encounter with a Rosary was more than I could handle. I began to gasp for breath. Shortly afterward, I found myself downstairs in the emergency room being treated for chest pain, while my baby was on the fifth floor in the fight of her life. I was given a sedative and released to go be with my daughter.

The next morning, she was taken off the vent, and she started breathing on her own. The breathing was labored and erratic, but it was breathing. About thirty minutes later, with my son, Chad, holding her one hand and me holding her other hand, my baby took her final breath. I kissed her face like there was no tomorrow because there was no tomorrow. She looked so peaceful as if she was in a deep, spellbound sleep.

As life left her body, emptiness filled mine. I felt as if someone was holding my head underwater.

It was so unfair.

I wished that I could trade places with her.

I wanted God to take me, not her. I had lived a great life. My baby had her whole life ahead of her.

It pained me to look at my son's face after Jordan died. His face was void of emotion or any normal expression. Jordan and Chad were best friends. He was a great brother to her. He gave her his car, sent her money, gave her crazy advice, and he always told her how beautiful she was. No matter his flaws, Jordan loved and respected Chad for who he is. When I would say something negative about Chad, she would say, "Ma, Chad has the best heart of anyone I know. You will not talk about my brother to me." She was serious. Chad was three years older than Jordan; but, I think Jordan acted more like his older sister much of the time.

As a mother, I had to deal with my pain and my son's pain. The fact that Chad had treated Jordan like a queen and had been such a wonderful brother to her, would serve him well in dealing with the pain, grief and the uncertainty that awaited him.

A Temporary Fix

Every morning for three months, I would drag myself, heavy from the aftermath of Xanax and Ambien, out of bed to my daughter's room, only to be greeted by the stuffed monkey on the made bed. My doctor had prescribed these drugs because sleep had become a stranger to me and my nerves were completely gone. The monkey's name was Caesar. Jordan loved the movie *The Planet of the Apes*. It was only fitting that when I gave it to her for Valentine's Day in 2011, she named him Caesar.

In July of 2013, four months after Jordan's funeral. I took my two bottles of pills and flushed them down the toilet. My temporary fix to mask my heartache was gone. Then I was forced to sit in my grief. I was forced to feel the pain from the grief. I cried like somebody was paying me to recycle my tears. I was an emotional wreck. I would announce to myself aloud "Your daughter is dead!" Every time that I would hear myself say that, I would get this uneasy feeling in my soul, but it was my way of beginning to face the reality that Jordan was gone forever.

I had no income. I had left my travel nursing job in San Antonio, Texas abruptly after Jordan collapsed. I had no daughter, and my son had gone back to Italy to continue his service in the United States Air Force. My ex-husband's body was there, but Jordan was our superglue. The marriage was becoming unglued, suddenly.

My ex-husband was a wonderful provider, honest, and hardworking, but expressing emotions seemed foreign and scary to him. He would always open the doors for me, but he never opened up emotionally. I needed him after Jordan died. I needed something from him that he did not have to give. I felt abandoned and alone.

I remembered the words of my late father, Cormac Parker Sr. Every time that I would call him for advice, he had an amazing way of motivating me. He once told me that I could eat an elephant, one bite at a time, and he was right. My belly was full of "elephant meat" when I walked across the stage to deliver my speech at our nursing pinning ceremony. I had finished nursing school, one bite at a time.

The challenge of losing a child would prove to be much more substantial than ingesting an elephant or the challenges of nursing school. To make matters worse, I did not have my dad there to guide and protect me, but I held on to his words. I could hear his deep voice in my head telling me that I would be okay. It was hard to believe at the time, but if Daddy said it, I would be okay.

Me, the Patient

After Jordan's death, I had to find a new space in this world without her. It was painful to imagine going forward without her beautiful face and massive energy. It has been said that energy never dies; but, that it transfers from one object to another. Where had Jordan's energy gone?

I was the nurse in the family. Who would nurse me in this desperate hour?

Over the years, while working as a registered nurse, I had grown accustomed to losing patients. I had given their families my "one day at a time" speech. I found myself repeatedly speaking aloud my father's words: "Tracie, you can do anything that you set your mind on."

People would tell me that they did not know what to say to me after I lost a child. I would always respond by saying that I did not know what to say to myself.

One day I guess I found the words. I was crying and talking . . . and laughing! I was plumb crazy. I was encouraging and nurturing my dang self! I began to pray to God because I needed help. I cried out, "Help me, God! You did this to me! Now, help me!" Burdened by all the crying, my eyes were red, swollen, and heavy, so I closed them. I had been assigned a new patient, me. I needed a visual assessment of this new patient.

Previously, my failed attempts at meditation would turn into prayer, but this time I found myself in full meditation mode. I was home alone, sitting on the floor in the television room. It took everything in me to stay focused, but I was meditating.

Eyes closed, I left my body and became two different entities. I, the nurse, stood there looking at this broken, grieving mother, me also, sitting criss-cross applesauce on the floor. Her pride was evaporated. She was sad, lonely, and scared. I focused heavily on her pain. It was so thick that it was palpable.

In that instant, I summoned the power of my pain like a superhero would channel his superpower to defeat evil. Grief was the villain, and it had me in a chokehold as I struggled to breathe. I repeated to myself, "Tracie, you are the strongest person I know!" I also repeated a verse from the Bible over and over and over until I believed every word. The verse was:

ature*I can do all things through Christ who strengthens me.*

—Philippians 4:13 (NKJV)

Through prayer, I had found my baby's energy. It was now accompanied by a newfound power that I had derived from pain. It was empowering and made me feel stronger, less sad, and more determined than ever to let Jordan's death make me instead of break me. I was bent, but I was far from broken. My very first successful meditation session had given me new life, energy, and power.

Superman had X-ray vision and was faster than a speeding bullet. The Incredible Hulk was huge, had limitless power and the Hulk Smash. Thor had the hammer. Prayer was my superpower. In the famous words of Uncle Ben (*Spider Man*), "With great power comes great responsibility!"

TRACIE HUNTER EVERS

Premonitions

There is no easy way to lose a child; however, I am comforted by the fact that my baby was a Christian. She dedicated her life to Jesus at the age of twelve and had recently gotten serious about her relationship with God. I was also consoled by our last conversation when she told me that it was the best day of her life.

A few weeks before her death, I started having nightmares. Every time it would end with a news broadcast about Jordan having been kidnapped. The dreams were frightening. I woke up each time with her heavy on my mind.

Because of the nightmares, I felt like it was me who was going to die. At the time, I was having terrible heart complications and was under a cardiologist's care. Back in 2012, I was admitted to Wake Forest Baptist Medical Center in Winston Salem, North Carolina, for three days after an episode of paroxysmal supraventricular tachycardia. I was working night shift at Baptist on a travel assignment. After exiting a patient's room, I felt a sudden pain in my chest. It felt like Mike Tyson had punched me in my torso. Sweating and short of breath, I sat on the floor in the hallway. I could feel my heart racing but was surprised to learn that my heart rate was hanging in the 180s. The normal resting heart rate is between 60 and 100 bpm. I was an inpatient for three days, and they ran multiple tests and labs. At the end of that hospitalization, they knew no more than they knew at the beginning.

Since the age of twenty-seven, I have visited the emergency room at least twice a year with chest pain. My chest was always hurting.

I made multiple trips to the local emergency room for chest pain, anxiety, or panic attacks in the months immediately before Jordan died. I felt like my spirit was disconnecting from my flesh. I phoned my son, Chad. Since he was my eldest child, I wanted to talk to him about what to do in the event of my untimely death. Chad wanted no parts of that conversation. He quickly said, "Ma, just tell all that stuff to Jordan. Get her to handle all of that."

I called Jordan. I was a little torn about placing the responsibility of handling my affairs, in the event of my death, on a twenty-year-old. I did not want to scare her, so I started the conversation off by telling her that I needed to give her some of my personal information for emergency purposes. First, I gave her my Facebook password and my bank account information. Then, I moved on to the heavier stuff. We talked about life insurance, funerals, life, death, and everything in between.

Jordan had been taking notes the entire time. I thought we were finished talking, but she asked me if I had something to write on. I told her no. She asked me to get pen and paper so she could give me her Facebook password and her bank account information. I just assumed that she was being polite. Then she chuckled and said, "If I die, I want y'all to wear purple." I laughed and told her that she was not going to die and that she would live to be a hundred years old. I jotted down her information on a scrap piece of paper and tossed it on my dresser, never expecting to actually need it. In the back of my mind, I felt it was quite strange that a college student would volunteer such personal data. When Jordan died, having her passwords definitely made my life easier than it would have been without them.

In the last dream, on the night before Jordan collapsed, my ex-husband and I had taken Jordan and two of her friends to the movies at a mall. In the theater, some strange guy arrived late and took the only seat remaining. It happened to be directly behind Jordan's seat. Periodically, during the movie, he would tap Jordan on the shoulder in response to something that took place on screen and say, "That was good, wasn't it?" or he would say "Yes!"

After he touched her a third time, I stood and shouted, "Sir, do not ever put your hands on my daughter again in life!"

He did not say another word, and he certainly did not touch her again. He just had this weird grin on his face. We got through the rest of the movie without further interruption. That guy was the first person to leave the theater after the movie ended.

Good riddance! I thought.

Because the movie theater was inside a mall, I voiced my interest in shopping, but the three young people looked disappointed. One of

Jordan's friends said that the movie was so good she wanted to watch it again. Jordan and the other friend quickly agreed.

We were outnumbered, so we agreed that they could watch the movie again while we shopped. We knew how much time we had because we had just spent an hour and a half watching it. The plan was to meet in that very same spot after they saw the movie for the second time.

When my ex-husband and I returned to the designated meeting spot, the girls were not there. Soon, patrons were no longer exiting the theater. Actually, the two-man cleanup crew was headed in. I started to wonder where the heck Jordan and the girls were. Just then, a security guard approached us and asked us to follow him. He escorted us to an office where a video was already playing. As soon as we entered the office, the security guard reached over and rewound the video. On the monitor, I could see a white van. Then I could see Jordan and the girls being forced into the van at gunpoint. But there was no one holding the gun. It was floating in the air as it directed the girls to enter the open sliding door. Once they were in, the van sped off. I was hysterical. They were never seen or heard from again.

The dream was so bad that it affected me physically. I awoke to chest pain, and I was struggling to breathe. Back to the emergency room I went.

In real life, Jordan was not missing. She was attending college at the University of South Alabama in Mobile, Alabama. It was only six o'clock in the morning, so it was too early to call her. As soon as the clock struck seven, I hurriedly picked up my cell and dialed her number. I called three or four times. There was no answer. Then, I remembered that Jordan had an early class that day and I thought perhaps she was doing some last-minute studying. I decided that I would attempt to call her later.

The early part of the day had passed. At two o'clock that afternoon, I picked up the phone and dialed Jordan's number again. In typical Jordan Seymone fashion, she answered, "Hey, Ma!"

I said, "Hey, lil girl, how was your day?" She was no little girl, but she was my baby, my everything.

SUMMONED

She seemed to be having a great day. She told me several times that it was the best day of her life. After hearing it a few times, I asked her why it was the best day of her life. She went on to inform me that "It just is, Ma. We have a volleyball game tonight, and we will win!"

After the dream I had, it was only natural as a mother to chastise her about safety. I told her to be careful and reminded her to stay away from strange people. Without giving details, I told her I had a dream about her, and I demanded that she never go near a van, any van. She responded with "Whoa, Ma! How is your day? Ma, if God gives you a dream, it is your dream. It's not for me. He gives me my own dreams!" Ironically, this "best day of her life" turned out to be one of the worst days of my life. Indeed, they won the game, but Jordan collapsed afterward and eventually died.

Jordan's cause of death was sudden cardiopulmonary arrest secondary to a lethal arrhythmia of unknown origin. The autopsy determined that Jordan's heart valves were faulty; but the coroner was not completely certain if her heart valves were malfunctioning before her death, or if it was caused by the medicines and procedures used to resuscitate her.

My mom had open heart surgery in 2017 because of a leaky mitral heart valve, and I recently underwent open heart surgery because of an ineffective and leaky mitral valve. Because of these events, it is likely for me to assume Jordan had the same affliction.

Numbers

I only recall Jordan having one fight while in high school, and that was because another basketball player was trying to take her jersey number, number 20. She wore that number on her softball jersey, her high school basketball jersey, and her very expensive Senior Letterman's jacket.

I do not believe for a second that it is a coincidence that Jordan died at the age of twenty because that was her favorite number.

The number 20 is an interesting number, between the last teen year and turning twenty-one and becoming an adult. I cannot explain it, but her dying at age twenty tells me her death was carefully orchestrated by the Creator.

> *To every thing there is a season and a time for every purpose under the Heaven. A time to be born and a time to die; a time to plant and a time to pluck up that which is planted; A time to kill and a time to heal; a time to break down and a time to build up; A time to weep and a time to laugh; a time to mourn and a time to dance.*
>
> —Ecclesiastes 3:1–4 (KJV)

> *A good name is better than precious ointment and the day of death better than the day of one's birth.*
>
> —Ecclesiastes 7:1 (KJV)

The number I find most interesting is Jordan's date of death—3/26/2013. It is absolutely no coincidence that her dad's birthday is in March (3), I was born on the twenty-sixth of February (26), and her brother was born on the thirteenth of June (13). I don't think that these numbers are special and that Jordan was special because she was my child. I know that she was special because she never belonged to me.

Jordan collapsed in a gym full of young people. That was divine intervention. God was using Jordan to touch the hearts of everyone who witnessed her collapse. He used Jordan to remind all of us affected by her death that death is coming. God is in control.

> *But of that day and hour knoweth no man, no, not the angels of heaven, but my Father only.*
>
> —Matthew 24:36 (KJV)

STAGE 2

ANGER

Anger is an understandable emotion when dealing with death, especially the untimely death of a child. It is a natural response to hurt and pain. No parent should ever have to bury their child.

ACTUAL JOURNAL ENTRY

8/28/2015

Dear Pain,

My pain on a scale of 1 to 10 is 1,000!

Why do you continue to hurt me over and over? You are a homewrecker. I have carried you on my back and held you in my grieving heart for some years now. I know you very well, yet we've never been formally introduced.

My name is Tracie Hunter Evers, the mother of Jordan. I am the recipient of the broken arm and shattered heart you sent with no return address.

You are energetic and bold. No matter how much you hurt me, you are the one who makes me feel most alive. You warn me of my body's weaknesses. You make me want to give away everything that

I have until there is nothing left of me to give . . . except you, and I would not give you to my worst enemy.

I want to let you know that you may motivate me at times as well as stall my efforts at other times, but God is the author and editor of my life. He orders my steps, not you.

It seems that you have zero conscience. How do you sleep at night?

Lose my latitudinal and longitudinal address because I never, ever want to see you again! I hate you! I wish you a slow and very painful death!

I miss my girl

Tracie Hunter Evers

Facebook Helped

I was mad as hell. I could not hide my anger from God because nothing is hidden from Him. But the people, I could smile for them even through this tragedy. I was still Tracie with the big smile. I was the strongest person they knew and the angriest person they would never get to see.

I had the regret of being in a position to write a book surrounding the death of my child. I would much rather have written about sunsets, lingering kisses and fantastic romances. Yet there I was, journaling and posting on Facebook about the events surrounding Jordan's life and death. It was my release.

After the loss of my beautiful twenty-year-old daughter, Jordan, Facebook served as a therapeutic outlet for my grief.

As a registered nurse, I had rehearsed this scenario over and over with my patients throughout the years. This time it was no rehearsal. Death had invaded my personal space. Pain was front and center and my bereavement unmasked for all to see. On this side of grief, there stood an uncomfortable and unimaginable reality. I had to do something.

Social media became an unlikely support system. Facebook became an altar. But God, He was still God.

Once the pills were gone, the anger came pouring down like the great flood. The unfairness was overwhelming, and nothing made sense on this side of Heaven. I was mad at the world. My only real connections to people were through my Facebook posts. My friends were very receptive to me writing about my grief, my pain and about me dealing with the loss of my daughter. I would post pictures of Jordan, post biblical scriptures and post prayers. I would get condolences and prayers in return. I needed that support more than the senders or even I realized at the time. I would share stories of our lives with them. I even shared my private poems I had written about Jordan after her death. Facebook was very salutary for me.

I was filled with rage, and being able to post about the memories of my daughter calmed me. I began receiving inbox messages via Facebook from strangers expressing to me how much I motivated them. Many mothers expressed that they were inspired to hug their daughters a little closer and to develop a more positive relationship with them.

TRACIE HUNTER EVERS

ACTUAL JOURNAL ENTRY

Carry On

I am anchored to this dirt,
My eyes read your name like a prayer
Carved in stone for time to test
My heart races, as if it can catch up to you
I wish we could trade places
I wonder if you would stand here
At my graveside and wish for me
The way my heart calls out for you
Would you be sad?
Would you harbor this deep never ending pain?
Would you hear my voice in your head?
Would you remember all that I taught you?
Would you smile at the memories?
Like they were friends waiting to greet you
Would they remind you to hold your head high,
Push your shoulders back
And carry on?
Would you remember to thank God for the twenty years
We had together?
Because in this moment,
On this side of the grave,
I know that I am.

Written by Tracie Hunter Evers

My Facebook Post (September 23, 2014)

Confirmation Tuesday! My child is in Heaven praying for me, so, whatever plans the devil thought he had for me today, got prayed away. We all learned how to pray at night, but never underestimate MORNING PRAYERS! Good morning, folks

My Facebook Post (March 26, 2014, one year anniversary of Jordan's death)

My heart is so full of memories of you. On this day, I choose to remember the good times and we had so many. I remember my ears ringing with gut-wrenching laughter. I remember the great fun, great food, the smiles, the hugs and the many lessons we learned together from just living our lives. I remember the spades battles that lasted, many times, throughout the night. I remember when you and Chad set those woods on fire. It was not funny at the time, but I laugh now, because I remember.

I will never forget the summer you, Chad and I spent living on the beach in Daytona, Florida. That was our little slice of Heaven on Earth. I know that it was no coincidence that you almost drowned there. Heaven was trying to take you then, but our love kept you a little while longer.

I also remember the summer that we spent in Houston, Texas and the month we spent in Omaha, Nebraska. I will always cherish our summer in Winston Salem, North Carolina.

You were silly; yet, brilliant. You lived more in twenty years than some people could dream of in a lifetime. Because you lived, you died.

I remember our photo shoots, our home-made talent shows and our hot dog eating contests. I remember how you and I could see something crazy and would struggle to not look at each other for fear of laughing and not being able to stop. I remember all the good times. I can sense your spirit and feel your energy and with that I am good.

I remember you being in my belly. I could not see you but I loved you. Now, you are in Heaven and I can no longer see you but I love you more than ever. Thank God for memories.

My Facebook Post (May 22, 2013)

I remember going to the walking track with my daughter. My goal was to walk around the track ten times and her goal was to run around the track ten times. I remember her flying past me, she was getting it. I also, remember her sitting on the bench waiting on me to finish. Just as in her life, she finished early. I remember having to walk the last two or three laps without her whizzing past me. I know that she is waiting in Heaven on me to finish my "walk."

Jordan's Facebook Post (January 30, 2013)

Don't tell God how big your problems are . . . tell your problems how big your God is.

Jordan's Facebook Post (January 17, 2013)

When you have God, you have no limits. Do not set your standards to those of the world if you were called to do or to be more.

Jordan's Facebook Post (January 15, 2013)

Even the rainiest days have a purpose.

Jordan's Facebook Post (January 8, 2013)

God probably just sits back and laughs when we worry about things. Pray more. Worry less.

Jordan's Facebook Post (November 18, 2012)

I refuse to settle for the world's standards. I am a child of God and will live by God's standards.

Jordan's Facebook Post (November 6, 2012)

If God isn't real, I don't know who is. I was going at least 70 mph down a hill and a black truck was creeping across the road and stopped in front of me. I missed them by not even a foot after slamming on my brakes. Lord, thank you for only giving me a headache and not giving my loved ones a heartache. Stop taking even the simplest things for granted and take time to count your blessings.

Jordan's Facebook Post (October 14, 2012)

Woke up smiling . . . Must be my Lord and Saviour. Everyone have a blessed day.

Jordan's Facebook Post (October 11, 2012)

I've learned not to question God's doings. He has a reason for everything and only time will tell why. Don't fret when you think everything's going wrong. It only means that something good is to come. Thank you Lord for giving me another day. Good Morning everyone and God bless!

Jordan's Facebook Post (September 28, 2012)

God's moving . . . Get ready.

Jordan's Facebook Post (September 18, 2012)

God puts people in our lives for a reason. He has blessed me with three amazing people that I thought I couldn't live without; but, then He separated me from them so I could realize that it is He who I cannot live without. At first, I thought He was punishing me but He's only doing his work. Thank you Lord for working on me! Just want to let these three know that I love them and I miss them greatly. God please continue to keep a hand over them. My mother, Tracie. My brother, Chad and my good friend, Kayla Farver.

Jordan's Facebook Post (August 5, 2012)

It really touches me when friends my age acknowledge God's work and thank Him for all He has done. Y'all really do encourage me to continue to build a stronger relationship with Him. Just wanted to take the time to let you know that your words are touching somebody. When praises go up, blessings come down.

Jordan's Facebook Post (July 11, 2012)

Stressed, but life is not meant to be easy. God puts us through situations to make us into the person He wants us to be. Like clay, the more we are squeezed and shaped, the better the finished product.

Jordan's Facebook Post (July 10, 2012)

Yeah, God is definitely up to something. Good night and sweet dreams everyone.

Jordan's Facebook Post (June 24, 2012)

Never underestimate the power of God. He may not deliver when you want it but He always delivers right on time.

Jordan's Facebook Post (April 19, 2012)

God is good all the time and all the time God is good.

Jordan's Facebook Post (April 12, 2012)

*Dear Devil,
God has been too good to me for me to give in to your ways now.*

Jordan's Facebook Post (March 4, 2012)

God makes no mistakes. He's brought me too far to leave me hanging now.

SUMMONED

Jordan's Facebook Post (January 25, 2012)

Even though I woke up with a little cold this morning, I have to give God his deserved praise because He didn't have to wake me up. With that being said, Good Morning everyone. Have a blessed day.

Jordan's Facebook Post (January 22, 2012)

Put God first and everything else will fall in place.

Jordan's Facebook Post (December 25, 2011)

Today isn't about getting the best gifts but praising the best God who has sacrificed the greatest gift . . . Merry Christmas

Jordan's Facebook Post (December 18, 2011)

No reason to stress, God won't give you anything that you can't handle.

Jordan's Facebook Post (December 14, 2011)

A relationship with God is the best relationship you can ever have.

Jordan's Facebook Post (October 24, 2011)

I can't live for anyone but God and myself.

Jordan's Facebook Post (September 12, 2011)

Dear God,
Although I cannot see the path ahead of me please guide my feet and faith in the right direction.

TRACIE HUNTER EVERS

Jordan's Facebook Post (July 21, 2011)

God may not answer your prayers when you want Him to but He always answers on time.

STAGE 3

BARGAINING

Bargaining has been identified by experts as the third stage in the process of grieving. Most of the time, God is the One Whom we make promises to in return for help. "God, You did this. Now please fix it. I will do anything to have my child back!"

End of the Rope

Although my first child was gifted to me when I was only eighteen years old, I had enough foresight to attend parenting classes. I even read old child psychology books left at our house by my aunt, Tajuana. By the time my youngest child was a sophomore in college, I had invested heavily in the moral preload of both my children, Chad and Jordan.

Chad and Jordan made motherhood easy. They were very good people. They were both kind, compassionate and loving children.

My marriage was not perfect, but it was working. It was working really well before Jordan's death. They say that the death of a child puts pressure on a relationship, and I guess that was true in our case.

I cannot remember a time in life that I ever wanted for anything that I did not get. I was my dad's only child for twenty years before my little brother and sister were born, and I have the kind of mother who always puts her two girls' wants and needs ahead of hers.

By all accounts, I had lived a wonderful life with plenty of favor from God. At the time of her death, Jordan was in college with her whole life ahead of her. We had talked about how she would join the Air Force and travel the world. She would never get that chance.

Jordan was excited about a new romance she had started with a young man named Aaron. I only met Aaron after Jordan was admitted to ICU. He was tall like Jordan and seemed very sweet. He would come to visit her daily between classes and after work. I imagined their life together. I imagined that Jordan had given me beautiful grandchildren and she lived to be a hundred years old. The reality was that Aaron had recently gotten a puppy and named him AJ, after his and Jordan's first initials. The pup was as close as I would get to having grandchildren from Jordan.

My prayers had turned into begging. I was begging God for a miracle. I remember the scene from *The Grey* with Liam Neeson. Liam's character, John Ottway, is at the end of his rope, his last friend had just drowned, and he turns to God and screams,

> "Do something! Do something! You phony prick! Fraudulent (BLANK)! Do something! Come on! Prove it! (BLANK) faith, earn it! Show me something real! I need it now! Not later, now! Show me, and I'll believe in you till the day I die. I swear. I'm calling on you. I'm calling on you! I'll do it myself. I'll do it myself."

ACTUAL JOURNAL ENTRIES

I stood in the doorway of the church to march in for my daughter's funeral. I felt faint. My knees felt like they could no longer hold the weight of my body, and I suddenly felt nauseous. I heard a clear voice from the heavens whisper, **"I got you!"**

March 30, 2013

I don't remember that actual ceremony, yet folks were coming up to me afterward, congratulating me for praising God during Jordan's funeral. Everyone was saying that I was strong. My thought was *Who, me?* Someone said that during the eulogy, the pastor called me out. He told the mourners, "If the mother can praise God at a time like this, that is the power of God! Right there!" as he pointed in my direction.

April 2, 2013

STAGE 4

DEPRESSION

In the depression stage of grieving, you actually see the effects of grief. It is usually exhibited as bouts of crying, insomnia, lack of interest in the normal activities of daily life, and an overall aura of hopelessness.

Sadness

Depression is a state of suspended sadness that can lead to clinical depression. Clinical depression is a serious medical illness that causes the individual to feel hopeless about who they are and where they are in life. When a person is clinically depressed, there are changes that happen chemically in the body, especially, in the brain.

There are numerous factors that affect how each person will be impacted by depression. If you had issues with depression before a significant loss, you are definitely going to be more prone to becoming clinically depressed. Some individuals seem to manage their depression with prescription medications that fall into the category of antidepressants; such as Zoloft, Prozac, Lexapro, Paxil, and Celexa.

Although medication can be a way to control mood swings in a depressed person, they come with a laundry list of potential side effects and adverse reactions.

I never considered myself depressed after Jordan died, but I was extremely angry. I was angry that I could no longer live my life with my daughter living her life. I witnessed other mothers fussing and fighting with their daughters on Facebook and in my family. I was mad. Jordan and I had long passed that phase of turmoil in our relationship.

Every time that I would meet a young lady and she would tell me that she did not speak to her mother, I wanted to slap her; however, I always kept my composure and prayed for strength.

I kept Jordan's cell phone on my nightstand, and I paid the bill every month for a long time. Sometimes I would dial her number and watch the phone vibrate until her voicemail picked up. I would always leave her messages, asking her to return my call.

For me, depression played out in my life as sarcasm and indignation.

I am a person who has always believed in treating people fairly. I could not understand why God was doing this to me. If I was being wronged by a human, I could curse them out or choose to never be around them again. I was not crazy enough to curse God, but I was very, very angry with Him, and He knew it.

There Is No Blueprint for Grief

Grief is a common emotion in the lives of everyday people and the pain derived from that grief is universal. Just as we are different as individuals, we all grieve differently. One's personality has a lot to do with how they grieve. If you are an introvert in your daily life, you will grieve as an introvert. Your personality will not change. If you are an extrovert, you may be more expressive during your grieving process. When you grieve, your life experiences, past hurts and pains, and the magnitude of the loss, as perceived by you, all affect how hard and how long you grieve.

When a person loses a loved one, one of the questions becomes "What is now missing along with the physical body that has been lost?" When a person loses a spouse, they also lose that person's income. They lose the intimacy they shared with them. They lose that companionship and their relationship status. They are no longer married.

When you bury your child, you bury all the hopes and dreams you had for them. You worked your butt off to make sure your child was safe and secure. You provided clothing, shelter, and unconditional love to that child. Your goal as a parent was to make sure that your child would be able to support themselves and become a contributing member of society. Therefore, you feel like a failure. Death has gotten in the way of your child being able to take care of himself or herself. You, most likely, had counseled and corrected that child's behavior. You are frustrated because death is beyond your scope of practice as a parent. You cannot correct your child's behavior of dying.

From the day my children were born, I prayed for them and for me to be a good mother to them. Never in a million years would I have imagined that God would take one of them so soon. If someone had told me that Jordan was going to die, I would have purchased seven straitjackets in seven different colors with matching heels for each day of the week.

Jordan had played basketball since she was eight years old. She played high school basketball, volleyball, tennis and ran track for Gautier High School in Gautier, Mississippi. She also played softball, and I had the pleasure of co-coaching her softball team. Jordan was very active. She was so alive.

Jordan died at twenty years old, and she had never been in love. We would never get to see our Jordan walk down an aisle to get married.

For me, the grief came in waves. Sometimes I would see something that would cause me to think about the "what-ifs" and the "what could have beens." There were times when memories of her would take me right back to the emotions I had immediately after her death. It has been five years since she died. I will never allow myself to be defined by grief.

Some people expected me to "get over" my daughter's death and move on. It does not matter if the child you lost was one day old, one year old, or twenty years old. A person never gets over the death of a child.

The worst thing you can say to a person who is grieving is to tell them that time heals all wounds. Time has not healed the wounds caused by Jordan's death. I will have this pain until the day I die, but I have God. Instead of focusing on the pain of Jordan's death, I have learned to focus on the energy derived from the pain.

Do not let other people determine how or how long you grieve. Cry. Do whatever you need to do when you are in a state of bereavement because there is no blueprint for grieving.

ACTUAL JOURNAL ENTRY

Jordan's senior year in high school was financially taxing. With her prom, letterman's jacket, senior portraits, class ring, and all the other expenses related to her senior year, we spent a couple thousand dollars on top of the normal expenses. Jordan said that when she graduated from college, she would start a scholarship for high school seniors. She would never get that opportunity. After she died, I knew exactly what type of scholarship I would start in her memory.

SUMMONED

My Yearly Facebook Post

ATTENTION: High School Students

SCHOLARSHIP OPPORTUNITY!!
Future high school graduates,
There will be many opportunities to pay for college by way of scholarships, loans and grants. Jordan's Random Acts of Kindness Scholarship, is for high school SENIORS.

How to apply:

1. *Have a teacher, coach, principal, or some other authority/ educator send an email attesting to the KINDNESS of your character to: jordangreerfoundation@yahoo.com!*
2. *Simple, one email could earn you a cash award of $1800 to help with expenses such as senior portraits, class ring, prom, senior trips, letterman jacket or whatever. You may choose to use this award towards your college education! It's your choice.*
3. *The deadline for emails is (TO BE ANNOUNCED) No exceptions!*
4. *Emails can be two lines, two paragraphs, two pages or however long it takes. If the educator is aware of a specific act of KINDNESS you have performed, obviously that email will bear more weight than one that is void of examples of your KIND heart.*
5. *The winner/winners will be asked to participate in the Random Acts of Kindness Day to be held in December every year. Specific date/time TBA. The $1800 cash scholarship will be awarded at that time. This scholarship may have a single recipient but no more than four recipients.*

TRACIE HUNTER EVERS

ACTUAL JOURNAL ENTRY

Angel

They said that you should model,
You were beautiful
They said that you should be in the WNBA,
You were tall and athletic
They said that you should be a doctor,
You were intelligent...

BUT
God said that you should be an
ANGEL
Enough Said !

Written by Tracie Hunter Evers

STAGE 5

ACCEPTANCE

At some point in the midst of your tragedy, you have to surrender to God. You have to trust him, even in the storm.

ACTUAL JOURNAL ENTRY

I had to listen to God because He was the only voice in my head giving out directions. I didn't have a plan A, B, or C. I had nothing but the voice. My grief had swallowed me whole like a hungry whale would a dog who had wandered too far out in the ocean. I was in a dark and desperate place, and if I were to be saved, it was to be God Himself who would rescue me.

February 26, 2016

The Mind

Thinking is having the ability to store, retrieve, and process information. From the moment that we are born, we learn, and we record all that we see, hear and do. The mind is life, and it is the place that the presence of God dwells within us.

God is in my mind and heart, and so is Jordan. I have never seen God, and I only have the memories of seeing Jordan, in my mind, the same mind where God is.

At some point throughout this process, I could feel myself growing spiritually. I came to the conclusion that we are all here to uplift the kingdom of God. We may have different careers, talents, strengths, weaknesses, and pains; but, we all have one solitary purpose: to serve God. I would get so frustrated when I would hear someone say they want to find their purpose in life.

Your purpose is to serve the Creator.

I do understand that as humans, we are fallible and struggle sometimes with the "how," but the "why" is so simple that many of us, even the devoutly religious folks, miss it.

At another point, there also came the realization that prayer and meditation were powerful tools that are underutilized.

At first, when I tried meditation, I would be wiggling like a two-year-old after about three minutes. Every time I tried to go to a quiet place to meditate, my mind would always drift towards the kitchen. I could focus best when food was the object of my focus. I've come up with some awesome recipes during my trials with meditation. I would most likely end up cooking full course meals at odd hours as a result of me attempting to meditate.

Meditation did not work for me all the time, but prayer did. It could be argued that prayer is just as effective as meditation as it relates to concentration and focus of the mind to control the actions of the body and to motivate the person to start a task.

Real faith is when you are able to pray knowing that your needs have already been met; yet, you pray with the sincerity and focus as if your needs have not been met. True enlightenment goes far beyond a visual confirmation into a realm of a supernatural verification.

As a registered nurse, I perform admission assessments on every new patient. This assessment is one part physical examination, one part questionnaire, and one part education. Because I was a travel nurse for a while, I have seen many different questionnaires with questions that each facility deemed important to ask a new patient during the admission process. One of the common questions was "Does your spirituality play a role in your decision-making in regards to your health?" In twelve years of nursing, only five of my patients answered no, and three of them were being admitted with altered mental status.

Prayer as a tool means that you are a Christian who believes in the almighty power of prayer. You believe that God is a healer and you have the faith to stand on His promises. The phrase "Jesus, take the wheel" comes to mind. Some say if you're gonna worry, do not pray, and if you are gonna pray, do not worry. You should pray the prayer of Jabez: "God, what can I do for you?"

Prayer puts the star player in the game. Bottom of the ninth inning, two outs, bases loaded... in a tie game . . . and here comes Jesus up to bat. When you choose to include prayer in your health and daily life, it's a game changer. God can heal a broken heart.

Prayer is the reason that my arms are not restrained and I am not confined to a rubber room.

ACTUAL JOURNAL ENTRIES

God Makes the Best Lemonade. I can do all things through Christ who strengthens me.

March 26, 2013

I have been driven many times to my knees by the overwhelming conviction that I had nowhere else to go.

—Abraham Lincoln

March 26, 2013

TRACIE HUNTER EVERS

How my relationship with God has changed

Some nights, I would start off praying and end up crying myself to sleep. Most nights, I would start off having a serious meltdown and end up praying like a maniac. Either way, God was in there. He was by my side. He gave me relief from my pain. In those dark months immediately after Jordan's death, God commanded me to love. Yes, love.

It may seem unusual to some that I would be given orders to love when the greatest subject of my love was lying in a cold and lonely grave with her chest filled with plastic bags and her eyes glued shut.

About six months after Jordan's death, I accepted a nursing travel assignment to Winston Salem, North Carolina. I had already completed an assignment there in 2012 that lasted a year. I needed familiarity. I had met some great people when I worked at Wake Forest Baptist Hospital on the previous assignment. I had gotten especially close to one of my coworkers, Mesha Bennet, and I was looking forward to seeing her and spending time with her.

I drove to Winston Salem alone so I could clear my head. My home was in Mississippi, at the time, and that was the first business trip since burying my child.

I was not really alone on that journey. Pain was there in the passenger seat, all buckled up and ready to ride or die. It was just me, my pain, and the many questions that filled my head at that time. During that trip, I repeatedly asked God, "Why?" Why had He taken my daughter, my youngest child, my baby? She was so nice, so beautiful, so smart, and so alive.

Needless to say, I arrived in Winston Salem with more questions and zero answers to any of the questions that I started the trip with. It just made no sense for God to do that to me. Although I was no saint, I could think of nothing that I could have possibly sown to be reaping all this heartache and pain.

I had been working in Winston Salem about a month, and I saw an old lady shuffling toward the bus stop as I drove down a road that I frequently traveled. I had noticed her before. She was a little, old, frail, lady who appeared as if she'd had plenty of better days. That day, I decided to stop and take a closer look at this lady.

As evil as it sounds, I was thinking that God should have taken her instead of Jordan. She looked like she was in her mid-eighties, and she was moving like a wounded turtle. She looked like she should not have been doing errands alone, and she watched her feet as she slid them across the sidewalk toward the bus stop.

I parked my car and approached the old lady and the other two people who were apparently waiting on the bus.

I said to the old lady, "Good morning."

She replied, "Morning."

"How are you?" I responded.

She shuffled her feet until her back was turned to me. I guess that was her way of telling me to stop talking to her. A closer look at her revealed that her clothes were dirty and her shoes were too big. Maybe that was why she walked like that so her shoes would not come off. I left that bus stop in tears. *Why didn't God take her instead of Jordan?*

To this day, I have not gotten an answer as to why God took Jordan and why he allowed that old lady to continue to live. The good news is I eventually realized that I do not need an answer. God took Jordan because he is God. If I trust God, I must trust Him completely.

I have gone through a tremendous spiritual journey, and my relationship with God has changed entirely from before Jordan's death. God has comforted me and stood in my grief with me. He has provided me with things that I didn't even know I needed or deserved. I did not deserve God's grace, and He showered me with it. I never earned the mercy that He so freely gave to me.

When you find that you are alone with your pain and feel as if you have no one to turn to, talk to God. Prayer works. Trust me, it has worked for me. No matter what you are going through, never forget who is really in charge. When you pray, come to God vulnerable and ready for Him to turn your weakness into His glory.

I cannot talk about gifts from God without mentioning the most precious gift that He gave. God sent His son into the world so that the world, through Him, might be saved.

> *For God did not send his Son into the world to condemn the world, but in order that the world be saved through him.*
>
> —John 3:17 (ESV)

Noah's Ark

I was performing random acts of kindness everywhere I could with anyone I could. I kept feeling the urge to not just feed the homeless, but to also eat with them, the ones who actually wanted to eat. So I would purchase food for them and myself. Many times, I would just sit on the ground next to them on the street and eat. Some of them would offer me their seat usually a bucket. I would usually accept. I did not want to offend a genuinely chivalrous man or woman. I did not like sitting with them, and it was reassuring that I could leave their reality of hopelessness and despair at any time. I could not imagine having to sit on the ground to eat my meals with no huge television, no air conditioning, no foot prop, no shelter, just the outdoors and food donated at the mercy of strangers.

One day I approached a homeless-looking older man standing on the corner near Macaroni Grill Restaurant.

I approached him, and he said, "Hey, ma'am. How are you?"

I said, "Hungry."

He told me that he had fruit in his empty-looking backpack and commenced to unzipping it. I stopped him quickly.

I said, "I need some meat, not fruit. Let's walk over here to Macaroni Grill and get some lunch."

He said, "How are we gonna pay . . . with my good looks?"

SUMMONED

I said, "I'm buying us lunch. It's on me."

He asked, "Why?"

I answered, "My lunch date stood me up, and I do not like eating alone."

Winter had come and shielded the stench from his body as we walked toward the restaurant. Once inside, his funk hit me like Mike Tyson hit his fiercest opponents. Immediately, it was a near knockout, but I was on a mission. The plan was to eat with this man. Although I would eat faster than I had in my entire life, I was determined to sit across from him and share a meal. I thought, *He cannot leave himself. At least I get to leave after this bout.*

The conversation was fantastic. I do not know if I was getting used to his smell, if the smell of garlic and bread was hiding it, or if his conversation was so interesting that I no longer focused on input from my olfactory senses. His name was Mike, and he told me that he used to be a dog trainer and a dog breeder but he had gone bankrupt after someone poisoned his dogs. I did not know if that was true or not. I just knew that I was sitting across the table from a very intelligent man who regaled me with vivid tales about the government, war, and religion.

Customers were staring at us. I was black and he was white. I was young, and he was much older. He was disheveled, and I had on cute jeans and a simple T-shirt, but I was clean. He spoke very loudly, revealing some type of handicap with his hearing. We were an odd couple. The waitress approached us with reluctance. She stood so far away from the table that passersby kept saying excuse me, excuse me. She would tuck her butt towards our table and quickly return to her comfort zone. She took our order and immediately returned with our drinks. I never saw that waitress again. Someone else from the wait staff brought out our food and eventually gave us our bill.

Out of the blue, Mike told me that I needed to start going back to church. I never told him I had stopped going to church years earlier. I knew that church was in my heart and not in a building. Years ago, I set out to do church on the street. I set out to live church, be a good person, and make God proud. I didn't need nosey, jealous and hypocritical church folk in my life.

The nerve of this man to tell me what I needed to do. I could guess that he was not going to anybody's church smelling like he was smelling, but he was attempting to tell me what to do and how to do it. It was definitely time for this lunch to end.

He said, "Do you remember the story of Noah's Ark?"

I said, "Of course."

He said, "You remember the story, right?"

I said, "Mmmm, hmm."

He said, "Bear with me, Tracie. Noah built that big ole ark. It was huge. It took him many, many years to build that ark, but he did it because God told him to. Also, he had his in-laws on the ark with him for all those years. I could not stand to be with any of my in-laws for more than an hour. Ha! All those animals, no running water. It had to be hot and stinky."

Just then, I started to smell the stench from Mike again.

He continued. "Noah had to be in a lot of doodoo. It had to be messy on that boat. Ha! But he was with God. When you go back to church, just think about Noah. Church folks can be messy, but it's better to be in the mess with God than to be out in the world without Him. God wants us to fellowship with one another."

Mission accomplished.

> ***Let the word of Christ dwell in you richly, teaching and admonishing one another in all wisdom, singing psalms and hymns and spiritual songs with thankfulness in your hearts to God.***
>
> —Colossians 3:16 (ESV)

Enlightenment

All glory be to God! Although my religious conviction was shaken, God was speaking to me. Eventually, I listened and followed His commands. No matter where my pain came from, it was never taking up more real estate in my head or heart than God. When my dad died, I focused more on my relationship with God. When my grandmother died, more God. When my child died, I focused so heavily on God that people were accusing me of not grieving properly.

After Jordan's death, about twenty-five people texted, called, or communicated to me over the course of about three years, that they had dedicated their lives to God in Jordan's memory. They were mostly young people. God used Jordan's death to bring people closer to Him. God used Jordan's death to bring me closer to Him.

In the end, I was grieving, yet I was in what I call spiritual house arrest. There were only two spirits allowed, mine and the Lord Almighty.

I lost my mind when Jordan died. I was angry and sarcastic, but I soon realized that if I was to come out of this grandstand of grief, I would have to give all my attention to God. Once I gave my tears and energy to God, my problems became insignificant. See, you do not have to *suffer alone. You do not have to pretend to be strong because there is an antidote for pain, and that is love.* But be careful. Love is the antidote for any and all your struggles, but it is not His love for you. It is your love for Him. Our pains are tremendous. Will we love God enough to turn our attention away from our pain, no matter how much that pain screams, waves, jumps, and summons us? Will we focus on God in those desperate hours? He has already shown you how much He loves you. It is your turn, in the midst of your pain, to show God how much you love Him.

Trust in the Lord with all thine heart and lean not unto thine own understanding. In all thy ways acknowledge Him and He shall direct thy paths.

—Proverbs 3:5–6 (KJV)

For I reckon that the sufferings of this present time are not worthy to be compared with the glory which shall be revealed to us.

—Romans 8:18 (KJV)

And God shall wipe away all tears from their eyes and there shall be no more death, neither sorrow, nor crying, neither shall there be any pain: for the former things are passed away.

—Revelation 21:4 (KJV)

And call upon Me in the day of trouble; I will deliver you and you shall glorify Me.

—Psalm 50:15 (ESV)

I called upon the Lord in my distress: the Lord answered me and set me in a large place.

—Psalm 118:5 (KJV)

The Lord is my shepherd: I shall not want.
He maketh me to lie down in green pastures: He leadeth me beside the still waters.

He restoreth my soul: He leadeth me in the paths of righteousness for His name's sake.
Yea, though I walk through the valley of the shadow of death, I will fear no evil: for Thou art with me: Thy rod and Thy staff they comfort me.
Thou preparest a table before me in the presence of mine enemies; Thou anointest my head with oil: my cup runneth over.
Surely goodness and mercy shall follow me in all the days of my life and I will dwell in the house of the Lord forever.

—Psalm 23:1–6

Ahdris Jordan

The agony from the pain of Jordan's death is the worst feeling anyone can attempt to imagine. The feeling is like you have just gotten off a really tall and fast roller coaster ride, yet your feet never left the ground. I get a weird, queasy feeling in my stomach every time I think, *My girl is really dead!*

Five years have passed, and I try hard to focus on Jordan's life instead of her death. I am thankful for all the wonderful memories I have of her and with her. We were a happy family. The house was always filled with laughter, great food, bad dancing, and horrible singing. I am also blessed to have beautiful pictures of Jordan to remember her. She was gorgeous.

In stark contrast to the pain from Jordan's death is another feeling I had never imagined, and that is the feeling of becoming a first-time grandmother.

My grandson, Ahdris Jordan, was born on July 2, 2017, and he is absolutely perfect. Someone needs to come up with another word to describe how I feel about him because the word "love" is not big enough.

Because my son, Chad, is stationed in Italy, I have not seen my grandchild in person. I have only seen him on video chats via Facebook and in pictures. He is so big, strong, and smart. When I think of Ahdris, all I feel is joy, an unexplainable joy. I loved him before he was even thought of by his mom and dad, and I will make certain that he always feels love from me.

The duality of day and night, of good and evil; and, in this case, of agony and joy is the very nature of life and death. As we breathe twenty or so breaths per minute, experiencing the very definition of life, we must also acknowledge the opposing reality of our eventual death. One day there will be no breaths and no minutes.

ACTUAL JOURNAL ENTRY

Lie Down

Suddenly there is little air
Lie Down.
Suddenly you are queasy and afraid
An acute fear of falling quickly overwhelms you
Sometimes, you have to go crazy just to understand
What it's like to be sane
Lie down.
Tears fill the empty space
I sacrificed my all
Now my all is the pile of dirt at my feet
And I can only hope that one day we can both have peace
Lie Down

Written by Tracie Hunter Evers

MOVING FORWARD

In mid-2017, I was at the end of my nursing shift at Hendrick Medical Center in Abilene, Texas, and was giving report to the oncoming nurse. Suddenly, my vision became blurred and then completely black. I was standing at the nurse's station at the time, and just before things went black, I saw my manager, Ellen, sitting at the desk. In the calmest voice that I could, I said to her, "Can you finish my report because I'm about to die?" She asked me if I was serious and quickly rolled one of the chairs to position it behind me. As soon as my butt hit the chair, I started having sharp chest pain accompanied by shortness of breath. I truly believed that I was about to die. My daughter had died at twenty years old, so it was not unreasonable, in that moment, to dread my own death.

My coworkers called a rapid response for me. A rapid response is an emergency code used in medical care settings, usually in hospital settings. A team of professionals, including ICU nurses, respiratory therapists, lab workers, nursing supervisors, and the charge nurse from that unit, go in to assess a patient who is deteriorating to prevent them from going into cardiopulmonary arrest, preventing a code blue. It is an effort to respond to potential code blue situations before the patient meets the criteria to actually call a code blue. Usually, a code blue is called if the person is no longer breathing or breathing inadequately or if their heart is no longer beating.

I was attended to by the members of our rapid response team and transferred via stretcher to the emergency room department. In the ER, they performed lab work, vital signs, and other diagnostic tests specific to my presentation of chest pain. I was in the ER for about three hours, and my symptoms had completely resolved. I was told by the physician that I needed to follow up with my cardiologist the following Monday. That was a Thursday. I went to my first appointment with Dr. McClish, one of the local cardiologists in Abilene, on Monday. Dr. McClish was youthful, knowledgeable, and energetic. I was impressed. He performed a physical assessment on me. When he listened to my heart sounds, I saw the look of surprise on his face. He was not expecting that.

He said, "You have a pretty significant heart murmur."

I said, "Yeah, I know."

He told me that I needed to get an echocardiogram relatively soon to evaluate the cause of the murmur. An echocardiogram is a diagnostic procedure that uses ultrasound waves to visualize the structure of the heart and hear abnormal sounds of the heartbeat and valves. After the echo was completed, I returned back to Dr. McClish's office about a week later to get the results. When he came into the exam room, he looked concerned. He told me that my mitral valve, the heart valve that lies between the left atrium and the left ventricle of the heart, was leaking and that I needed open heart surgery.

Surprisingly, I was not scared, but I was numb. From the moment that I heard those words "You have to have open heart surgery," I let God do the worrying. I had enough to worry about before this new diagnosis. My mother had open heart surgery a few months earlier. She was still recovering. I was still dealing with Jordan's death. My son, Chad, was stationed overseas, and I constantly worried about him. My divorce was pending. I had moved across country to a new state and started a new job. Yes, you could definitely conclude that my plate was full.

Dr. McClish referred me to a cardiothoracic surgeon in Dallas, Texas. His name was Dr. Poole.

Dr. J. Mark Poole is a very talented cardiothoracic surgeon. This man was such a blessing to me and my family. He was more than my doctor. He was also a prayer partner and a friend. God used Dr. Poole to heal me, and I will forever be indebted to God and to Dr. Poole.

My mother's surgery was in Biloxi, Mississippi, in April of 2017 and it went well. She is doing very well, but she has a huge scar down the middle of her chest. I do not have that scar. There are no scars down the middle of my chest. Dr. Poole performed a minimally invasive open heart surgery on me, where he gained entry underneath my right breast. So to see my scar, you have to lift my right breast and look really hard. This man had magic hands. For the surgery, I had to have the pacer wires and a chest tube. I also had tubes in my neck, I had to be on a heart and lung machine, and I was on a ventilator. But God has blessed me so good (yes, I said so good) that folks are doubting my blessings of health and healing. They doubt the almighty power of God. When I returned to work three months after surgery, two of my coworkers were questioning if I even had open heart surgery. I overheard one of them say, "She looks too good, and she's moving too fast. I do not believe that she had open heart surgery. Look at her chest. There is no scar."

I smiled.

TRACIE HUNTER EVERS

A Letter from my cardiac surgeon

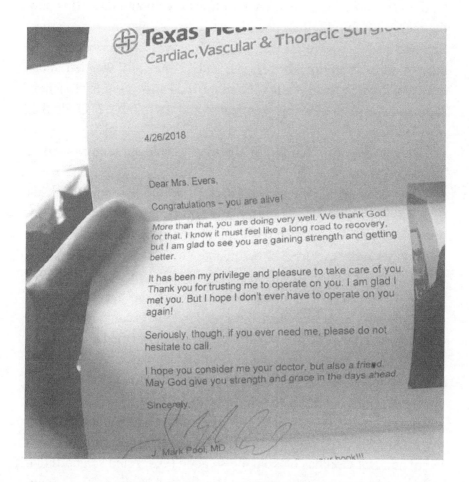

Now

One of the most stressful things that I did was in April of 2018, about one week after heart surgery. I cut my hair. I did the big chop. I had long hair past my shoulders, but there was damage from years of perms, heat, and hair colorings. I decided to trust God even with my hair. Cutting my hair was liberating and empowering. It was similar to the power I had derived from prayer and meditation.

On this new journey, I am focusing on the inner me, the real me, and the spiritual me. I am embarking on a new journey in a new state, new city, new job, new home, new church, new friends with a new man. I got a divorce from the first husband and married someone whom I met at seventeen years old and had not seen in quite a few years. Jay Evers is my soulmate, best friend, and the love of my life. God has been preparing us separately to be together now. I have been renewed.

I was baptized in the Church of Christ on Meridian Street in Moss Point, Mississippi, as a child at the urging of my aunt, Johnnie Mae Hunter. For the past couple of years, there has been this voice in my spirit telling me to get baptized again. So on May 16, 2018, I was baptized into the Church of Christ on Minda Street in Abilene, Texas. This second baptism was a totally different experience. The first time that I was baptized, I was terrified. The second time, I was excited, and I felt totally prepared. I have a new church home.

Someone is in Heaven praying for me

One of my nurses, when Jordan was born, was Catholic, and one of the nurses who took care of Jordan before she died in 2013 was also Catholic. For the longest time, I considered Catholicism because I felt as if God was trying to tell me something and that He was using Catholics to tell me.

I remember taking care of a monk in 2014 who told me that Jordan was in Heaven praying for me. He did not call her name, but he told me that she is praying for me. Before that moment, I had never thought about someone in Heaven praying. I never told him that my daughter was dead. I asked my coworkers if they had told the monk that my child was dead. Neither of them admitted to doing so. So I asked him if anyone told him my daughter was dead. He replied, "No." He said that I, actually, had two children in Heaven. The Monk said the female Angel was always praying for her mama and the male Angel was always praying for peace.

I have never, ever discussed with anyone the child that I lost before Chad or Jordan were born. That encounter with the monk was overwhelming. I left work early that day. I went by the public library and checked out several books on Catholicism. To this day, I am fascinated with the religious practices and study habits of people of the Catholic faith.

Guilt

Until recently, I felt this huge regret in my spirit surrounding Jordan's death. The very night she collapsed, I had a serious talk with God. I could not go be with my child in Mobile, Alabama, in that critical time because there were no available flights. All I could do was pray. I trusted God, so I ended that very first prayer with "May Your will be done." After she died, I did not want His will to be done. I wanted my child to be alive and well. Period. Why didn't I act a fool like I did in Daytona when she almost drowned? Why didn't I scream at the top of my lungs and beg God for a miracle? Why didn't I ask God to change His "will" if that meant that Jordan would die? I am a fighter. I felt like I should have fought more. I should have pleaded more. I should have prayed more.

I, eventually, realized that I did exactly what I was supposed to do. I set up counsel with God. I told Him how much I trusted Him and needed Him. Then I thanked Him. Jordan never belonged to me.

There is hope, and though life may not seem like it now, you will be okay. There is life after the tragedy.

—Tracie Hunter Evers

Jordan Seymone

PICS

October 16, 1992 - March 26, 2013

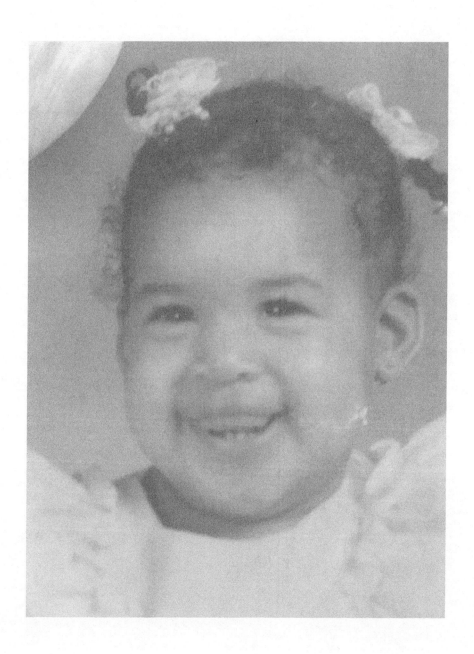

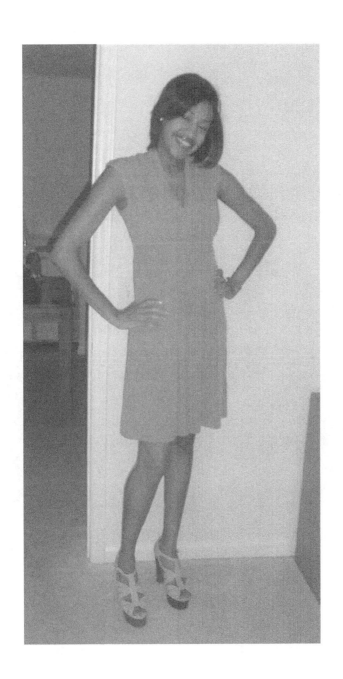

My favorite picture of Jordan and I

Chad and Jordan Pics

Jordan with Friends and Family Pics

Jordan's Legacy Of Kindness

GOD BLESS